SEO

A Beginner's Guide

2023
DOBBS MEDIA

Table of Contents

SEO: A Beginner's Guide 2

Understanding SEO Basics 5

Keyword Research 10

On-Page SEO Explained 16

Off-Page SEO 21

Technical SEO 27

Content Creation 33

User Experience (UX) 38

Analytics and Monitoring 43

Local SEO for Local Businesses 50

SEO Best Practices 57

SEO Tools 62

Common SEO Mistakes to Avoid 68

Resources for Learning SEO 73

SEO: A Beginner's Guide

In the ever-expanding digital landscape, where information flows like a mighty river, standing out and being discovered can seem like an elusive quest. Imagine having the power to make your voice heard, your products found, and your content seen amidst the vast ocean of the internet. Welcome to the world of Search Engine Optimization, or SEO.

This beginner's guide is your compass to navigate the dynamic and complex terrain of SEO. Whether you're a curious novice taking your first steps into the digital realm or a seasoned professional looking to solidify your understanding, this guide is your essential companion on the journey to mastering the art and science of SEO.

Unlocking the Digital Doorway

At its core, SEO is the key that unlocks the doorway to the digital world. It's the secret language that search engines like Google, Bing, and Yahoo understand. These digital gatekeepers are your partners on this journey, tirelessly sifting through the vast expanse of the internet to deliver the most relevant results to users' queries. And with SEO, you can ensure that your content, whether it's a website, a blog post, or an online store, receives the attention it deserves.

Your Path to Online Success

Imagine the potential: Your website appearing at the top of search engine results, attracting hordes of interested visitors, and converting them into loyal customers or avid readers. SEO can make this vision a reality. It's about understanding the rules of the digital game and using them to your advantage.

In this beginner's guide to SEO, we will embark on an exciting journey. We'll start with the fundamental concepts, ensuring that you have a strong foundation to build upon. We'll then delve into practical strategies and tactics, demystifying topics like keywords, on-page optimization, and link building. We'll explore the importance of user experience, mobile-friendliness, and content creation. Together, we'll decode the SEO puzzle.

The Ever-Changing Landscape

One thing to keep in mind as we set out on this journey is that the digital landscape is constantly evolving. Search engines refine their algorithms, user behaviors change, and new technologies emerge. Staying up-to-date is not just a recommendation; it's a necessity. This guide will equip you with the timeless principles of SEO while emphasizing the importance of adaptability in this dynamic field.

So, whether you're a small business owner looking to boost your online presence, a blogger aiming to reach a wider audience, or a student eager to explore the world of digital marketing, this beginner's guide to SEO is your roadmap. Let's embark on this enlightening journey into the heart of SEO, where the possibilities are as vast as the digital universe itself.

Understanding SEO Basics

Search Engine Optimization (SEO) is a critical component of modern digital marketing and web presence management. In this section, we will delve into the fundamental aspects of SEO, including what it is, why it's essential, and how search engines work.

What is SEO?

SEO is the acronym for "Search Engine Optimization." It is a multifaceted strategy and set of practices aimed at improving a website's visibility in search engine results pages (SERPs). The primary goal of SEO is to enhance a website's organic (non-paid) ranking for specific keywords and phrases relevant to its content or products. In simpler terms, SEO helps your website appear higher up in search engine listings when users search for information related to your site's content.

Why is SEO Important?

1. Increased Visibility:

- The majority of internet users turn to search engines (e.g., Google, Bing, Yahoo) to find information, products, or services. If your website is not optimized for search engines, it might not appear in relevant search results, leading to reduced visibility among potential visitors.

2. Organic Traffic:

- SEO is an effective way to attract organic traffic, which is traffic that comes to your website naturally through search results. Unlike paid advertising, organic traffic doesn't require ongoing ad spend, making it a cost-effective long-term strategy.

3. Credibility and Trust:

- Websites that rank higher in search results are often perceived as more credible and trustworthy by users. SEO can help establish your website as an authority in your niche or industry.

4. Better User Experience:

- SEO involves optimizing various aspects of your website, including content, design, and navigation. These improvements enhance the overall user experience, leading to higher user satisfaction and engagement.

5. Competitive Advantage:

- Many of your competitors are likely investing in SEO. By optimizing your website, you can stay competitive and potentially surpass them in search rankings, gaining a larger share of the market.

6. Data-Driven Insights:

- SEO tools and analytics provide valuable data on user behavior, keyword performance, and more. This data can inform your marketing strategies and help you make informed decisions.

How Search Engines Work?

Understanding how search engines operate is fundamental to grasping the concept of SEO. While the exact algorithms used by search engines like

Google are closely guarded secrets, the following overview outlines the basic process:

1. Crawling:

- Search engines use automated bots, often called "crawlers" or "spiders," to browse the internet and discover web pages. These crawlers follow links from one page to another, indexing the content they find.

2. Indexing:

- Once a page is crawled, search engines analyze its content, including text, images, and other media. They then catalog this information in massive databases, creating an index of web pages.

3. Ranking:

- When a user enters a search query, the search engine's algorithms assess the indexed pages to determine which ones are most relevant to the query. Various factors influence this ranking, including keywords, backlinks, and user engagement metrics.

4. Displaying Results:

- The search engine presents the most relevant results on the SERP, typically with the highest-ranked pages at the top. Users can then click on the search results to access the respective web pages.

5. Ongoing Updates:

- Search engines continually update their algorithms to provide more accurate and relevant results. This means that SEO efforts must adapt to algorithm changes to maintain or improve rankings.

In summary, SEO is the art and science of optimizing your website to align with the criteria search engines use to rank web pages. By understanding these basics and implementing effective SEO strategies, you can improve your website's visibility, attract more visitors, and achieve your online goals.

Keyword Research

Keyword research is a crucial component of search engine optimization (SEO). It involves identifying and selecting specific words and phrases (keywords) that people use when searching for information, products, or services online. In this section, we'll explore what keywords are, the tools available for keyword research, and the concept of long-tail keywords.

What Are Keywords?

Keywords are the words or phrases that individuals enter into search engines when seeking information. These keywords are the bridge between what people are looking for and the content your website provides. To grasp the importance of keywords, consider the following points:

1. Relevance:

- Keywords should be directly related to the content, products, or services offered on your website. Using relevant keywords helps attract users genuinely interested in what you provide.

2. Search Volume:

- Some keywords are searched for more frequently than others. Researching keywords with substantial search volume can help you target a larger audience.

3. Competition:

- High-demand keywords often have high competition among websites trying to rank for them. Balancing search volume with competition is essential for effective keyword selection.

4. User Intent:

- Understanding the intent behind a keyword search is crucial. Users may be looking for information, products, services, or specific actions (e.g., making a purchase). Align your content with the user's intent.

Tools for Keyword Research

Several tools are available to assist with keyword research. These tools provide valuable data to help you identify the right keywords for your SEO strategy. Some popular keyword research tools include:

1. Google Keyword Planner:

- A free tool by Google that provides keyword suggestions, search volume data, and competition levels. It's a great starting point for beginners.

2. SEMrush:

- A comprehensive SEO tool that offers keyword research, competitor analysis, and other valuable insights. SEMrush can help you uncover keyword opportunities and track your rankings.

3. Moz Keyword Explorer:

- Moz's tool provides keyword suggestions, search volume, difficulty scores, and SERP analysis. It helps you assess the competitiveness of keywords.

4. Ahrefs Keywords Explorer:

- Ahrefs offers a robust keyword research tool with search volume, keyword difficulty, and

SERP analysis. It's known for its backlink analysis capabilities as well.

5. KeywordTool.io:

- This tool generates keyword suggestions from Google's autocomplete feature, making it useful for finding long-tail keywords.

6. Answer the Public:

- This tool provides keyword ideas in the form of questions, prepositions, and alphabetical listings, helping you understand user intent better.

Long-Tail Keywords

Long-tail keywords are longer, more specific keyword phrases that typically consist of three or more words. Here are some key points to understand about long-tail keywords:

1. Less Competition:

- Long-tail keywords usually have lower competition because they are more specific. This makes it easier to rank for them.

2. Higher Conversion Rates:

- Users searching with long-tail keywords often have a clearer intent, which can lead to higher conversion rates. For example, someone searching for "best budget-friendly digital cameras under $500" is likely closer to making a purchase than someone searching for "digital cameras."

3. Niche Targeting:

- Long-tail keywords allow you to target specific niches within your industry. This can be valuable if you offer niche products or services.

4. Voice Search:

- With the rise of voice-activated devices and voice search, long-tail keywords are becoming more important. People tend to use natural, conversational phrases when speaking to voice assistants.

Incorporating long-tail keywords into your SEO strategy can be a smart move, especially if you're in a competitive market. These longer, more specific phrases can help you reach a highly targeted audience and drive qualified traffic to your website.

In conclusion, keyword research is a foundational step in SEO. By understanding keywords, using the right tools, and considering the value of long-tail keywords, you can optimize your website's content to align with what your target audience is searching for, ultimately improving your chances of ranking well in search engine results.

On-Page SEO Explained

On-Page SEO is like fine-tuning individual web pages to boost their visibility in search engine results while delivering a user-friendly experience. Let's delve into key aspects of on-page SEO with real-world examples:

1. Title Tags

What are Title Tags? Title tags are HTML elements that define a web page's title and show up as clickable headlines in search results and on browser tabs.

Example: Suppose you run a website selling handcrafted jewelry. Your homepage's title tag could be:

<title>Handcrafted Jewelry | Artisan Creations | YourBrand</title>

2. Meta Descriptions

What are Meta Descriptions? Meta descriptions are brief HTML snippets summarizing a web page's content, displayed beneath the title in search results.

Example: For your handcrafted jewelry product page:

<meta name="description" content="Explore our exquisite handcrafted jewelry collection, featuring unique designs and high-quality materials.">

3. Header Tags (H1, H2, etc.)

What are Header Tags? Header tags structure content, indicating headings and subheadings. H1 represents the main heading, followed by H2, H3, and so on.

Example: For an article about jewelry care:

<h1>Ultimate Guide to Jewelry Care</h1>

<h2>1. Cleaning Your Jewelry</h2>

<h3>1.1 Using Gentle Cleaning Solutions</h3>

4. Content Optimization

What is Content Optimization? Content optimization means crafting high-quality, informative content that is both user-friendly and search engine-friendly.

Example: In your blog post about gemstone selection:

- Use natural keyword integration: "When choosing gemstones for your handcrafted jewelry, consider the color, clarity, and cut."

- Maintain readability: Use short paragraphs, bullet points, and subheadings.

5. Image Optimization

What is Image Optimization? Image optimization involves reducing image file sizes without compromising quality for faster page loading and better user experience.

Example: For a product image of a handcrafted sapphire ring:

<img src="sapphire-ring.jpg" alt="Handcrafted Sapphire Ring" title="Handcrafted Sapphire Ring - Elegant Blue Jewelry">

6. URL Structure

What is URL Structure? URL structure refers to how web page addresses (URLs) are organized for SEO and user clarity.

Example: For a page about custom-made engagement rings:

- Good URL: **yourbrand.com/custom-engagement-rings**
- Bad URL: **yourbrand.com/?page_id=123**

7. Internal Linking

What is Internal Linking? Internal linking involves adding hyperlinks within your site's content, guiding users to other relevant pages on your website.

Example: In your jewelry blog post discussing gemstone types, you can link to a product page for each type mentioned: "Explore our exquisite ruby rings," linking to the ruby rings product page.

By optimizing title tags, meta descriptions, header tags, content, images, URL structure, and internal linking, your website can improve search rankings and provide an excellent user experience. Remember, successful on-page SEO is an ongoing effort, requiring regular updates and optimizations to stay competitive in search results.

Off-Page SEO

Off-Page SEO is a crucial aspect of search engine optimization that focuses on activities and strategies outside your website to improve its visibility and authority. In this section, we'll explore the key components of Off-Page SEO, including backlinks, link-building strategies, social signals, and online reputation management.

1. Backlinks

What are Backlinks?

Backlinks, also known as inbound links or incoming links, are hyperlinks from other websites that point to pages on your site. Search engines view backlinks as votes of confidence in your content and website's authority.

Example: If a reputable jewelry blog links to your handcrafted jewelry store's product page, it's considered a backlink. This tells search engines that your content is valuable.

Why are Backlinks Important?

- **Authority**: High-quality backlinks from authoritative websites can enhance your website's authority and trustworthiness.

- **Traffic**: Backlinks can drive referral traffic from other sites to yours.

- **Search Rankings**: Search engines often use backlinks as a ranking factor. Quality backlinks can help improve your search engine rankings.

2. Link Building Strategies

What is Link Building?

Link building is the process of acquiring high-quality, relevant backlinks to your website from other websites. It's an essential Off-Page SEO strategy.

Link Building Strategies:

- **Guest Posting**: Write valuable guest posts for authoritative websites in your niche, including a link back to your site.

- **Broken Link Building**: Identify broken links on other websites and offer your content as a replacement.

- **Resource Link Building**: Create comprehensive, informative resources that other websites would want to link to.

- **Outreach**: Reach out to website owners or bloggers in your industry and ask for backlinks.

- **Content Promotion**: Share your content on social media, forums, and communities to attract natural backlinks.

- **Partnerships**: Partner with other businesses or websites for cross-promotion and backlink opportunities.

3. Social Signals

What are Social Signals?

Social signals refer to the impact of social media activity on your website's visibility in search results. This includes likes, shares, comments, and overall social engagement with your content.

Example: When your jewelry blog post receives numerous shares and likes on Facebook, it sends a signal that your content is engaging and relevant.

Why are Social Signals Important?

- **Increased Visibility**: Social media engagement can lead to increased visibility as more people discover and share your content.

- **Traffic**: Social signals can drive traffic directly from social media platforms to your website.

- **Brand Awareness**: Active social media engagement can enhance brand awareness and loyalty.

4. Online Reputation Management

What is Online Reputation Management?

Online reputation management involves monitoring and influencing how your brand is perceived online. It includes managing online reviews, addressing customer feedback, and maintaining a positive online presence.

Online Reputation Management Strategies:

- **Review Monitoring**: Regularly monitor online reviews on platforms like Google My Business, Yelp, and social media.

- **Engagement**: Respond promptly and professionally to both positive and negative reviews.

- **Quality Customer Service**: Provide excellent customer service to encourage positive reviews and address issues before they become negative reviews.

- **Content Creation**: Create valuable, informative content that showcases your expertise and builds a positive reputation.

- **Social Media Management**: Maintain active and positive social media profiles that align with your brand's values.

Why is Online Reputation Management Important?

- **Trust and Credibility**: A positive online reputation builds trust and credibility with potential customers.

- **Competitive Advantage**: Managing your online reputation can give you a competitive edge in your industry.

- **Customer Retention**: Addressing issues promptly can lead to customer retention and repeat business.

In summary, Off-Page SEO plays a pivotal role in improving your website's visibility, authority, and reputation. By focusing on backlinks, implementing effective link-building strategies, nurturing social signals, and managing your online reputation, you can enhance your website's overall SEO performance and gain a competitive edge in the online landscape.

Technical SEO

Technical SEO focuses on optimizing the technical aspects of your website to improve its visibility and performance in search engines. In this section, we will explore the key components of technical SEO, including mobile-friendliness, site speed, XML sitemaps, robots.txt, and schema markup.

1. Mobile-Friendliness

What is Mobile-Friendliness?

Mobile-friendliness refers to how well your website performs and displays on mobile devices, such as smartphones and tablets. Given the prevalence of mobile users, search engines prioritize mobile-friendly websites in their rankings.

Importance of Mobile-Friendliness:

- Improved User Experience: A mobile-friendly design ensures that visitors on mobile devices can easily navigate your site, read content, and interact with it.

- Search Engine Rankings: Google uses mobile-friendliness as a ranking factor, meaning mobile-friendly sites tend to rank higher in mobile search results.

Example: If your jewelry website is mobile-friendly, it will adapt its layout and content to provide an optimal experience for users on smartphones and tablets, making it easier to browse and shop for jewelry.

2. Site Speed

What is Site Speed?

Site speed refers to how quickly your website loads and responds to user interactions. Fast-loading pages enhance user experience and are favored by search engines, which may boost your rankings.

Importance of Site Speed:

- User Experience: Faster loading times lead to a better user experience, reducing bounce rates and increasing engagement.

- SEO Rankings: Search engines like Google take site speed into account when determining rankings.

Example: If your jewelry website loads slowly, potential customers may become frustrated and leave before making a purchase. On the other hand, a fast-loading site encourages them to explore your products and complete transactions.

3. XML Sitemaps

What are XML Sitemaps?

XML sitemaps are files that provide search engines with a roadmap of your website's structure and content. They list all the URLs on your site, helping search engines index your pages more efficiently.

Importance of XML Sitemaps:

- Improved Indexing: Sitemaps ensure that search engines discover and index all of your website's pages.

- Crawl Efficiency: Search engine bots use sitemaps to understand the hierarchy and priority of your content.

Example: Your jewelry website's XML sitemap will list all the product pages, blog posts, and other content, making it easier for search engines to find and display relevant results to users.

4. Robots.txt

What is Robots.txt?

Robots.txt is a text file placed in your website's root directory to instruct search engine crawlers on which pages to crawl and index and which to exclude. It's used to control the behavior of web crawlers.

Importance of Robots.txt:

- Control Indexing: Robots.txt helps you prevent search engines from indexing certain parts of your site that you don't want to appear in search results.

- Avoid Duplicate Content: It can prevent search engines from indexing multiple versions of the same page, which can harm your SEO.

Example: If you have a login page or a development area on your jewelry website that you don't want to appear in search results, you can use a robots.txt file to block access to these areas for search engine crawlers.

5. Schema Markup

What is Schema Markup?

Schema markup (or structured data) is a code added to your website's HTML that provides search engines with additional context about your content. It helps search engines understand the type of content and may result in rich snippets in search results.

Importance of Schema Markup:

- Enhanced SERP Listings: Schema markup can lead to more informative and visually appealing search results, attracting more clicks.

- Better Understanding: Search engines can better understand the content and context of your pages, improving relevance in search results.

Example: If you're running an online jewelry store, using schema markup for product pages can provide details like price, availability, and customer reviews directly in search results, making your listings more appealing to potential buyers.

In conclusion, technical SEO is essential for optimizing your website's performance and ensuring it's accessible and user-friendly. By focusing on mobile-friendliness, site speed, XML sitemaps, robots.txt, and schema markup, you can enhance your website's technical foundation, leading to improved search engine rankings and a better user experience for your visitors.

Content Creation

Content creation is a fundamental component of a successful digital marketing and SEO strategy. High-quality, relevant content not only engages your audience but also plays a crucial role in improving your website's search engine rankings. In this section, we will delve into key aspects of content creation, including the importance of high-quality content, content relevance, blogging and content strategy, and how to avoid duplicate content issues.

1. High-Quality Content

What is High-Quality Content?

High-quality content is informative, valuable, and engaging material that satisfies the needs and interests of your target audience. It should be well-researched, well-written, and visually appealing.

Importance of High-Quality Content:

- **Audience Engagement**: Engaging content keeps visitors on your site longer and encourages them to explore more.

- **Authority Building**: High-quality content positions you as an authority in your niche or industry.

- **Search Engine Rankings**: Search engines, such as Google, reward high-quality content with better rankings.

Example: If you run a jewelry blog, high-quality content would include in-depth articles about the latest jewelry trends, expert guides on selecting gemstones, and visually appealing galleries of your jewelry collections.

2. Content Relevance

What is Content Relevance?

Content relevance refers to how well your content aligns with the interests, needs, and search intent of your target audience. Relevant content answers their questions and provides solutions to their problems.

Importance of Content Relevance:

- **User Satisfaction**: Relevant content ensures that visitors find what they're looking for, enhancing their satisfaction.

- **Search Engine Rankings**: Search engines aim to deliver the most relevant results to users, so relevance is a significant ranking factor.

Example: If your jewelry website's blog posts include articles about jewelry care, styling tips, and industry trends, they are considered relevant to your audience of jewelry enthusiasts.

3. Blogging and Content Strategy

What is Blogging and Content Strategy?

Blogging involves regularly creating and publishing new content on your website's blog. A content strategy is a plan that outlines what content to create, when to publish it, and how to promote it.

Importance of Blogging and Content Strategy:

- **Fresh Content**: Regularly updating your website with blog posts keeps it fresh and encourages search engines to crawl it more often.

- **Audience Engagement**: Blogging allows you to connect with your audience, address their questions, and provide value.

- **Long-Term SEO**: A well-executed content strategy can lead to long-term SEO benefits as your content ranks and attracts traffic over time.

Example: Your jewelry website's content strategy may include creating monthly blog posts about new jewelry collections, jewelry care tips, and customer stories to engage your audience and boost SEO.

4. Duplicate Content Issues

What are Duplicate Content Issues?

Duplicate content refers to identical or substantially similar content that appears on multiple pages within your website or across different websites. Duplicate content can harm SEO by confusing search engines and leading to lower rankings.

How to Avoid Duplicate Content Issues:

- **Canonical Tags**: Use canonical tags to indicate the preferred version of a page when you have similar content on multiple pages.

- **301 Redirects**: Implement 301 redirects to consolidate multiple versions of a page into a single, canonical URL.

- **Unique Content**: Ensure each page has unique, valuable content that serves a specific purpose.

Example: Avoid using the same product descriptions for multiple jewelry items on your online store. Instead, create unique descriptions for each piece to avoid duplicate content issues.

In conclusion, content creation is a cornerstone of a successful online presence. By consistently producing high-quality, relevant content, implementing a well-thought-out content strategy, and addressing duplicate content issues, you can enhance your website's visibility, engage your audience, and establish your authority in your niche or industry. Effective content creation is an ongoing process that pays off in improved SEO rankings and a loyal, satisfied audience.

User Experience (UX)

User Experience (UX) refers to the overall experience that visitors have when interacting with your website. A positive UX is vital for retaining visitors, encouraging engagement, and improving search engine rankings. In this section, we will explore the key aspects of UX, including mobile responsiveness, page layout and design, navigation and user-friendliness, and page speed optimization.

1. Mobile Responsiveness

What is Mobile Responsiveness?

Mobile responsiveness means that your website is designed and optimized to function seamlessly on various devices, including smartphones and tablets. With the increasing use of mobile devices, a responsive design is crucial for a positive user experience.

Importance of Mobile Responsiveness:

- **Wider Reach**: A mobile-responsive site ensures that you reach and engage with users on all devices.

- **Lower Bounce Rates**: Mobile users are more likely to stay and explore a site that is easy to navigate on their device.

- **SEO Benefits**: Google prioritizes mobile-friendly sites in its search rankings.

Example: A jewelry website with mobile responsiveness will adapt its layout, images, and navigation to provide an optimal experience for users on both desktop and mobile devices.

2. Page Layout and Design

What is Page Layout and Design?

Page layout and design encompass the visual presentation and organization of your website's content, including the arrangement of text, images, colors, and other elements. A well-designed website enhances user engagement and conveys professionalism.

Importance of Page Layout and Design:

- **First Impressions**: A visually appealing design creates a positive first impression and encourages users to explore further.

- **Content Readability**: A well-organized layout makes it easy for users to read and understand your content.

- **Branding**: Consistent design elements reinforce your brand's identity and credibility.

Example: A jewelry website might use a clean, elegant design with high-quality images to showcase its products, making it visually appealing and encouraging visitors to explore its offerings.

3. Navigation and User-Friendliness

What is Navigation and User-Friendliness?

Navigation refers to how users move through your website, find information, and access various sections. User-friendliness involves making the navigation intuitive and easy to understand, even for first-time visitors.

Importance of Navigation and User-Friendliness:

- **Reduced Bounce Rates**: Intuitive navigation helps users find what they're looking for, reducing bounce rates.

- **Increased Engagement**: Easy navigation encourages users to explore more pages and engage with your content.

- **Customer Satisfaction**: A user-friendly experience leads to satisfied visitors who are more likely to return.

Example: A jewelry website should have clear menu items like "Necklaces," "Earrings," and "Rings," making it easy for visitors to browse different product categories.

4. Page Speed Optimization

What is Page Speed Optimization?

Page speed optimization involves improving the loading times of your website's pages. Faster loading pages provide a better user experience and are favored by search engines.

Importance of Page Speed Optimization:

- **User Satisfaction**: Fast-loading pages keep visitors engaged and prevent them from leaving due to slow load times.

- **SEO Benefits**: Search engines use page speed as a ranking factor, so faster sites may rank higher.

- **Mobile Experience**: Mobile users, in particular, expect speedy page loading.

Example: A jewelry website should optimize image sizes, use browser caching, and employ content delivery networks (CDNs) to ensure that product images and pages load quickly for a seamless user experience.

In conclusion, user experience (UX) is a critical factor that can significantly impact the success of your website. By focusing on mobile responsiveness, page layout and design, navigation and user-friendliness, and page speed optimization, you can create a website that not only attracts visitors but keeps them engaged and satisfied, ultimately leading to improved search engine rankings and long-term success. A positive UX is an investment that pays off in increased user retention and conversions.

Analytics and Monitoring

Effective SEO relies on data-driven insights to make informed decisions and continuously improve your strategy. In this section, we'll explore the key components of analytics and monitoring in SEO, including setting up Google Analytics, monitoring keyword rankings, analyzing website traffic, and tracking conversions.

1. Google Analytics Setup

What is Google Analytics?

Google Analytics is a free web analytics tool offered by Google. It provides valuable insights into your website's performance, including user behavior, traffic sources, and more. Setting up Google Analytics is a crucial first step in SEO monitoring.

Steps to Set Up Google Analytics:

1. **Sign Up**: Create a Google Analytics account by visiting the Google Analytics website.

2. **Property Setup**: Add your website as a property and follow the setup instructions.

3. **Tracking Code**: Implement the unique tracking code provided by Google Analytics on every page of your website.

4. **Data Collection**: Google Analytics will start collecting data, which you can access through your account.

Importance of Google Analytics:

- **Traffic Analysis**: It helps you understand where your website traffic comes from, including organic search, referral sites, social media, and more.

- **User Behavior**: You can track user behavior on your site, such as page views, time on site, and bounce rates.

- **Conversion Tracking**: Google Analytics allows you to set up and track specific goals and conversions, such as form submissions or e-commerce transactions.

2. Monitoring Keyword Rankings

What is Keyword Ranking Monitoring?

Monitoring keyword rankings involves tracking the positions of your website's pages in search engine results pages (SERPs) for specific keywords. This helps you assess your SEO performance and make adjustments as needed.

Tools for Keyword Ranking Monitoring:

- **Google Search Console**: It provides information about how your site ranks for various keywords in Google.

- **Third-Party SEO Tools**: Tools like SEMrush, Ahrefs, and Moz offer comprehensive keyword ranking tracking features.

Importance of Keyword Ranking Monitoring:

- **Performance Assessment**: Regular monitoring allows you to evaluate the effectiveness of your SEO efforts.

- **Competitor Analysis**: You can also track how your site ranks compared to competitors for specific keywords.

- **Identifying Opportunities**: Identifying keywords that are rising in rank can help you focus your SEO efforts strategically.

3. Traffic Analysis

What is Traffic Analysis?

Traffic analysis involves studying the flow of visitors to your website, including where they come from, what pages they visit, and how long they stay. Understanding your website's traffic patterns can guide your SEO strategy.

Important Metrics in Traffic Analysis:

- **Source/Medium**: Identifies where your traffic is coming from, such as organic search, social media, or referral websites.

- **Pageviews**: Shows which pages are the most popular on your site.

- **Bounce Rate**: Indicates the percentage of visitors who leave your site after viewing only one page.

- **Session Duration**: Measures how long users spend on your site.

Importance of Traffic Analysis:

- **Content Optimization**: Helps you identify which content resonates most with your audience.

- **Conversion Opportunities**: Pinpoints where users drop off or engage, helping you optimize for conversions.

- **SEO Insights**: Allows you to see the impact of SEO changes on traffic and user behavior.

4. Conversion Tracking

What is Conversion Tracking?

Conversion tracking involves monitoring and measuring specific actions that you want users to take on your website, such as filling out a contact form, making a purchase, or subscribing to a newsletter.

Steps for Conversion Tracking:

1. **Set Goals**: Define what constitutes a conversion on your website (e.g., a completed purchase).

2. **Configure in Google Analytics**: Use Google Analytics to set up goals or e-commerce tracking for specific conversions.

3. **Implement Tracking Code**: Place tracking codes on relevant pages to track conversions.

4. **Analyze Data**: Monitor the conversion data in your analytics tool.

Importance of Conversion Tracking:

- **Performance Assessment**: Helps you gauge the effectiveness of your website and marketing efforts.

- **ROI Measurement**: Allows you to determine the return on investment for various marketing campaigns.

- **Optimization**: Identifies areas for improvement to increase conversion rates.

Example: If you have an online jewelry store, conversion tracking can help you measure how many users complete a purchase and which products are most popular among buyers.

In conclusion, analytics and monitoring are essential for maintaining and optimizing your SEO strategy. By setting up Google Analytics, monitoring keyword rankings, analyzing website traffic, and tracking conversions, you can gather valuable insights that will guide your SEO efforts, identify areas for improvement, and ensure that your website continues to perform well in search engine rankings while meeting your business goals.

Local SEO for Local Businesses

Local SEO is a vital digital marketing strategy for businesses that serve specific geographic areas. It focuses on optimizing your online presence to ensure your business appears prominently in local search results. In this section, we'll explore key components of local SEO for local businesses, including Google My Business, NAP consistency, local citations, and online reviews.

1. Google My Business

What is Google My Business?

Google My Business (GMB) is a free tool provided by Google that allows businesses to create and manage their online presence, particularly on Google Search and Google Maps. It's a critical component of local SEO.

Steps to Optimize Google My Business:

1. **Claim or Create Your Listing**: If your business isn't already listed, claim it, or create a new listing.

2. **Complete Your Profile**: Fill out all relevant information, including business name, address, phone number, hours of operation, categories, and photos.

3. **Verify Your Listing**: Google may require verification through mail, phone, or email.

4. **Regular Updates**: Keep your GMB listing updated with current information, such as holiday hours or special offers.

5. **Engage with Reviews**: Respond to customer reviews, both positive and negative, in a professional and timely manner.

Importance of Google My Business:

- **Local Visibility**: A well-optimized GMB listing helps your business appear in local search results.

- **Information Accuracy**: Provides users with accurate and up-to-date information about your business.

- **Customer Engagement**: Allows customers to leave reviews, ask questions, and connect with your business.

2. NAP Consistency

What is NAP Consistency?

NAP stands for Name, Address, and Phone number. NAP consistency refers to ensuring that your business's name, address, and phone number are consistent across all online platforms, directories, and listings.

Importance of NAP Consistency:

- **Search Engine Trust**: Consistent NAP information builds trust with search engines, leading to higher rankings.

- **Customer Trust**: It helps customers find and contact your business easily.

- **Accurate Citations**: Accurate NAP information is crucial for local citations (next point).

Example: If your business is listed as "ABC Jewelry Store" with the address "123 Main St., Suite 100" and the phone number "(555) 123-4567" on your website, this same information should be used consistently across all online listings.

3. Local Citations

What are Local Citations?

Local citations are online mentions of your business's NAP information. These citations can appear in various places, including online directories, social media profiles, and review websites. Consistent citations signal to search engines that your business is legitimate and relevant to local searchers.

Steps to Build Local Citations:

1. **Identify Relevant Directories**: Find local and industry-specific directories where you can list your business.

2. **Ensure NAP Consistency**: Use the same NAP information on all citations.

3. **Complete Profiles**: Fill out as much information as possible on each platform.

4. **Monitor and Update**: Regularly check for inaccurate or outdated citations and update them.

Importance of Local Citations:

- **SEO Boost**: Citations help improve your website's authority and visibility in local search results.

- **Local Trust**: Consistent citations build trust with local customers.

- **Competitive Advantage**: Citations can give you an edge over competitors in local searches.

4. Online Reviews

What are Online Reviews?

Online reviews are feedback and comments left by customers on platforms such as Google, Yelp, Facebook, and industry-specific review sites. They play a significant role in influencing potential customers and impacting your local SEO.

Tips for Managing Online Reviews:

1. **Encourage Reviews**: Ask satisfied customers to leave reviews on relevant platforms.

2. **Respond Promptly**: Address both positive and negative reviews in a professional and courteous manner.

3. **Monitor Reviews**: Regularly check and respond to reviews to show that you value customer feedback.

4. **Use Reviews for Improvement**: Use feedback to improve your business's products and services.

Importance of Online Reviews:

- **Trust Building**: Positive reviews build trust and credibility with potential customers.

- **Ranking Factors**: Reviews can influence local search rankings.

- **Customer Insights**: Reviews offer insights into what customers like and dislike about your business.

Example: Positive reviews from satisfied jewelry customers can encourage others to choose your store when searching for jewelry in your area.

In conclusion, local SEO is essential for local businesses looking to attract nearby customers. By optimizing your Google My Business listing, ensuring NAP consistency, building local citations, and managing online reviews, you can improve your online visibility, credibility, and reputation in your local community, ultimately driving more customers to your business. Local SEO is an ongoing effort that can lead to long-term success and growth for your local business.

SEO Best Practices

Search Engine Optimization (SEO) is an ever-evolving field with a set of best practices designed to improve a website's visibility in search engine results. To succeed in SEO, it's crucial to understand the difference between white hat and black hat SEO, follow ethical guidelines, and stay updated with search engine algorithms.

1. White Hat vs. Black Hat SEO

White Hat SEO

- **Ethical**: White hat SEO practices adhere to search engine guidelines and ethical standards.

- **Long-Term Focus**: White hat SEO strategies prioritize sustainable, long-term results.

- **Content-Centric**: High-quality content, keyword optimization, and user-focused strategies are at the core of white hat SEO.

Examples of White Hat SEO:

- Creating valuable and informative content.

- Optimizing meta tags and title tags.

- Earning backlinks through outreach and content quality.

- Improving website speed and user experience.

Black Hat SEO

- **Unethical**: Black hat SEO tactics involve practices that manipulate search engine algorithms to gain higher rankings, often violating guidelines.

- **Short-Term Gains**: Black hat SEO may yield quick results, but they are usually short-lived and can lead to penalties or bans from search engines.

- **Keyword Stuffing**: Overloading content with keywords, hidden text, and spammy backlinks are common black hat techniques.

Examples of Black Hat SEO:

- Cloaking: Showing different content to search engines and users.

- Buying low-quality backlinks in bulk.

- Content scraping and duplicate content.

- Clickbait and deceptive tactics.

2. SEO Ethics

Ethical SEO practices are essential for building a sustainable online presence and maintaining a positive reputation. Ethical SEO involves:

- **Transparency**: Be transparent with your audience about your products, services, and affiliations.

- **Honesty**: Provide accurate and honest information to users.

- **Respect for Guidelines**: Respect search engine guidelines and avoid any tactics that may lead to penalties or bans.

- **User-Centric Approach**: Prioritize the needs and interests of your audience over short-term gains.

- **Avoiding Deception**: Do not use deceptive practices to mislead users or manipulate search engine rankings.

Ethical SEO not only helps you build trust with your audience but also ensures long-term success in your online efforts.

3. Staying Updated with Search Engine Algorithms

Search engines, such as Google, frequently update their algorithms to provide better search results and combat spammy practices. To maintain and improve your SEO performance, you should:

- **Follow Industry News**: Stay informed about the latest developments in the SEO industry through reputable sources, blogs, and forums.

- **Google's Webmaster Guidelines**: Regularly review and adhere to Google's Webmaster Guidelines, which provide insights into best practices.

- **Algorithm Updates**: Be prepared for algorithm updates and their potential impact on your website's rankings.

- **Experiment and Adapt**: Test and adapt your SEO strategies based on algorithm changes and user behavior.

Search engine algorithms consider various factors, including content quality, user experience, mobile-friendliness, and backlink quality. Staying updated allows you to adjust your SEO tactics to align with these evolving criteria.

In conclusion, adhering to white hat SEO practices, maintaining ethical standards, and staying updated with search engine algorithms are essential for a successful and sustainable SEO strategy. A long-term approach focused on providing value to users, creating high-quality content, and following ethical guidelines will lead to better rankings, increased trust with your audience, and ultimately, improved online success.

SEO Tools

SEO tools are essential for optimizing your website's performance, analyzing data, and making informed decisions to improve your search engine rankings. In this section, we will explore some of the most important SEO tools, including SEO plugins for content management systems (CMS) like WordPress, keyword research tools, and backlink analysis tools.

1. SEO Plugins (For CMS like WordPress)

What are SEO Plugins?

SEO plugins are extensions or add-ons that you can install on your website, typically within a CMS like WordPress. These plugins enhance your site's SEO capabilities by providing tools and features to optimize on-page SEO elements and improve overall website performance.

Examples of Popular SEO Plugins:

- **Yoast SEO**: Yoast SEO is a widely used WordPress plugin that helps optimize content, meta tags, XML sitemaps, and more.

- **All in One SEO Pack**: This plugin offers features like XML sitemaps, meta tags optimization, and social media integration.

- **Rank Math**: Rank Math is known for its advanced SEO capabilities, including schema markup and redirection management.

Key Features of SEO Plugins:

- **Meta Tag Optimization**: Plugins assist in optimizing title tags, meta descriptions, and header tags for better on-page SEO.

- **XML Sitemaps**: They generate and submit XML sitemaps to search engines for efficient indexing.

- **Content Analysis**: Some plugins provide content readability and keyword density analysis.

- **Schema Markup**: Advanced plugins offer schema markup options to enhance rich snippets in search results.

2. Keyword Research Tools

What are Keyword Research Tools?

Keyword research tools help you identify and analyze the search terms and phrases that potential visitors use to find content or products related to your business. Effective keyword research is a fundamental aspect of SEO.

Examples of Popular Keyword Research Tools:

- **SEMrush**: SEMrush offers comprehensive keyword research, competitor analysis, and rank tracking features.

- **Moz Keyword Explorer**: Moz provides keyword research insights, including search volume, difficulty, and SERP analysis.

- **Google Keyword Planner**: Google's free tool provides keyword ideas and search volume data.

Key Features of Keyword Research Tools:

- **Keyword Suggestions**: Tools offer keyword suggestions based on your niche, allowing you to discover relevant search terms.

- **Search Volume**: You can assess the popularity of keywords and their potential traffic.

- **Keyword Difficulty**: Analyze the competition level for specific keywords.

- **SERP Analysis**: Some tools provide insights into the search engine results pages (SERPs) for specific keywords.

3. Backlink Analysis Tools

What are Backlink Analysis Tools?

Backlink analysis tools allow you to monitor and evaluate your website's backlink profile. They provide insights into the quantity and quality of backlinks, helping you identify opportunities for link building and improving your website's authority.

Examples of Popular Backlink Analysis Tools:

- **Ahrefs**: Ahrefs is a comprehensive SEO tool that offers in-depth backlink analysis, competitor research, and keyword tracking.

- **Majestic**: Majestic provides a detailed view of your backlink profile, including Trust Flow and Citation Flow metrics.

- **SEMrush**: In addition to keyword research, SEMrush offers backlink analysis features, including backlink audits and competitor backlink analysis.

Key Features of Backlink Analysis Tools:

- **Backlink Discovery**: These tools identify and list all the websites linking to your site.

- **Quality Assessment**: Assess the quality and authority of backlinks using metrics like Domain Authority (DA) and Trust Flow.

- **Competitor Analysis**: Analyze your competitors' backlink profiles to identify link-building opportunities.

- **Backlink Monitoring**: Track changes in your backlink profile over time and receive alerts for new or lost backlinks.

In conclusion, SEO tools play a crucial role in optimizing your website for search engines. SEO plugins for CMS platforms like WordPress simplify on-page optimization, keyword research tools help you identify valuable search terms, and backlink analysis tools allow you to monitor and improve your website's authority. Combining these tools with effective SEO strategies can significantly enhance your website's search engine rankings and overall online presence.

Common SEO Mistakes to Avoid

While optimizing your website for search engines is crucial for online success, there are several common SEO mistakes that can hinder your efforts. In this section, we'll explore these mistakes and provide guidance on how to avoid them.

1. Keyword Stuffing

What is Keyword Stuffing?

Keyword stuffing is the practice of excessively and unnaturally incorporating keywords into your website's content, meta tags, or alt text in an attempt to manipulate search engine rankings. This practice not only provides a poor user experience but can also result in search engine penalties.

How to Avoid Keyword Stuffing:

- **Focus on User Intent**: Create content that genuinely addresses user queries and provides value.

- **Natural Language**: Use keywords naturally within your content, aiming for readability and relevance.

- **Variety of Keywords**: Diversify your keyword usage by including synonyms and related terms.

- **Avoid Overuse**: Avoid repeating keywords excessively within the same piece of content.

2. Ignoring Mobile Optimization

What is Mobile Optimization?

Mobile optimization involves ensuring that your website performs well and provides an excellent user experience on mobile devices, such as smartphones and tablets. Ignoring mobile optimization can lead to reduced rankings and user frustration.

How to Avoid Ignoring Mobile Optimization:

- **Responsive Design**: Implement a responsive design that adapts your website's layout and content to different screen sizes.

- **Page Speed**: Optimize your website's loading times on mobile devices.

- **Mobile-Friendly Testing**: Use Google's Mobile-Friendly Test to identify and resolve mobile compatibility issues.

3. Neglecting User Experience

What is Neglecting User Experience?

Neglecting user experience (UX) involves creating a website that doesn't prioritize the needs and preferences of your visitors. Poor UX can result in higher bounce rates and decreased rankings.

How to Avoid Neglecting User Experience:

- **Intuitive Navigation**: Ensure easy navigation with a clear menu structure and a logical layout.

- **Mobile-Friendly Design**: Prioritize mobile responsiveness for a seamless experience on all devices.

- **Quality Content**: Create high-quality, valuable content that satisfies user intent.

- **Page Speed**: Optimize your site for fast loading times to prevent user frustration.

4. Not Tracking and Analyzing Results

What is Not Tracking and Analyzing Results?

Failing to monitor and analyze your SEO efforts means missing out on valuable insights and opportunities for improvement. Without data analysis, you won't know if your strategies are working or where to make adjustments.

How to Avoid Not Tracking and Analyzing Results:

- **Set Up Analytics**: Implement tools like Google Analytics and Google Search Console to track website performance and search rankings.

- **Regular Monitoring**: Monitor your website's traffic, keyword rankings, and user behavior regularly.

- **Data Analysis**: Analyze the data to identify trends, strengths, weaknesses, and areas for improvement.

- **Adjust Strategies**: Use data-driven insights to refine your SEO strategies for better results.

In conclusion, avoiding these common SEO mistakes is essential for achieving and maintaining strong search engine rankings and providing an optimal user experience. By focusing on creating valuable content, using keywords naturally, optimizing for mobile devices, prioritizing user experience, and tracking and analyzing results, you can establish a solid foundation for your SEO efforts and avoid the pitfalls that can hinder your online success.

Resources for Learning SEO

Learning SEO (Search Engine Optimization) is essential for improving your website's visibility on search engines like Google. Fortunately, there are numerous resources available to help you develop your SEO knowledge and skills. In this section, we'll explore three key types of resources for learning SEO: blogs and websites, online courses, and SEO communities and forums.

1. Blogs and Websites

Blogs: Many SEO experts and organizations maintain blogs that provide valuable insights and updates on SEO trends and techniques. These blogs are excellent sources of information, especially for staying current with the ever-changing SEO landscape.

- **Moz Blog** (https://moz.com/blog): Moz is a well-known SEO software company that offers a blog filled with in-depth articles, guides, and industry insights. They cover everything from beginner's guides to advanced SEO strategies.

- **Search Engine Land**
  (https://searchengineland.com): Search Engine
  Land is a reputable source for news and analysis
  of the search marketing industry. Their articles
  cover a wide range of SEO topics and provide
  expert opinions.

Websites: Aside from blogs, there are websites
dedicated to SEO education. For example, Google
provides an official guide called the "Search Engine
Optimization (SEO) Starter Guide," which is a
fantastic starting point for beginners.

- **Google's SEO Starter Guide**
  (https://support.google.com/webmasters/answ
  er/7451184?hl=en): Google's guide covers the
  fundamentals of SEO, making it a great resource
  for those new to SEO.

2. Online Courses

Online courses offer structured, comprehensive
learning experiences for individuals who want to dive
deep into SEO. These courses are often self-paced
and come with various resources, including video
lectures, quizzes, and assignments.

- **Coursera** (https://www.coursera.org): Coursera offers courses on SEO, such as the "Search Engine Optimization (SEO) Specialization" by the University of California, Davis. This specialization covers SEO fundamentals, content strategy, and more.

- **Udemy** (https://www.udemy.com): Udemy hosts a wide range of SEO courses, including "SEO 2022: Complete SEO Training + SEO for WordPress Websites." These courses are created by industry experts and cover various aspects of SEO.

- **HubSpot Academy** (https://academy.hubspot.com): HubSpot provides a free SEO certification course that covers SEO strategy, on-page optimization, and link building. It's suitable for both beginners and experienced marketers.

3. SEO Communities and Forums

Being part of an SEO community or forum allows you to connect with other SEO enthusiasts, ask questions, share experiences, and stay updated with industry news. These platforms provide a space for discussions and networking.

- **Reddit - r/SEO** (https://www.reddit.com/r/SEO/): The SEO subreddit is a vibrant community where SEO professionals and beginners share insights, ask questions, and discuss the latest SEO trends.

- **Warrior Forum - SEO Section** (https://www.warriorforum.com/seo/): Warrior Forum has an SEO section where marketers discuss various SEO strategies, tools, and tactics. It's a platform for both beginners and experts.

- **WebmasterWorld** (https://www.webmasterworld.com/): WebmasterWorld is an SEO forum that covers a wide range of topics related to website management and SEO. It's a valuable resource for webmasters and SEO professionals.

By exploring these blogs, online courses, and SEO communities and forums, you can gain valuable knowledge, improve your SEO skills, and stay informed about the latest developments in the field. Whether you're a beginner or an experienced SEO practitioner, these resources offer opportunities for continuous learning and growth in the world of SEO.

"In the journey through the pages of this book, we've explored the intricate world of Search Engine Optimization (SEO). From its foundational principles to advanced strategies, we've embarked on a quest to unravel the mysteries of how websites rise to prominence in the digital realm.

We began with the fundamental understanding of what SEO is and why it matters. We learned that SEO is not merely about search engines but, more importantly, about delivering valuable experiences to users. We dived into the intricate world of keyword research, understanding how these digital signposts can shape the destiny of a website in the vast landscape of the internet.

On-page SEO became our compass, where we discovered the power of optimizing titles, descriptions, and content to communicate effectively with both search engines and human visitors. We explored the art of crafting compelling content and ensuring that images and URLs play their vital roles in the grand SEO symphony.

Off-page SEO introduced us to the world of backlinks, social signals, and online reputation management. We understood the significance of building trust and authority in the eyes of both search engines and our audience.

The realm of technical SEO beckoned, where we learned the importance of mobile-friendliness, site speed, XML sitemaps, and structured data. It was here that we embraced the unseen forces that propel websites to the forefront of search engine rankings.

We journeyed through the world of content creation, understanding that high-quality content is the lifeblood of SEO. We grasped the importance of relevance, strategy, and the perils of duplicate content.

User Experience (UX) became our lodestar, guiding us to create websites that are not only functional but also beautiful and efficient. We understood the profound impact of mobile responsiveness, page layout, and page speed on user satisfaction.

Analytics and monitoring became our watchtower, allowing us to measure the fruits of our SEO labor.

With tools like Google Analytics, we tracked keyword rankings, analyzed traffic, and fine-tuned our strategies to achieve better results.

For local businesses, we explored the realm of Local SEO, where Google My Business, NAP consistency, local citations, and online reviews were the pillars of success in the competitive local market.

As we conclude this SEO odyssey, let us remember that SEO is not a destination but an ongoing journey. The digital landscape is ever-evolving, and staying updated with search engine algorithms and best practices is paramount.

We hope that this book has been a valuable companion in your SEO journey, equipping you with the knowledge and skills needed to navigate the complex terrain of the online world. May your websites climb the ranks, delight your users, and achieve the success they deserve in the digital realm.

In the ever-shifting sands of SEO, remember that the quest for knowledge and the pursuit of excellence are your most potent allies. As you apply the principles and strategies learned within these pages, may your online presence shine brightly amidst the vast expanse of the World Wide Web.

Happy optimizing!"